CALIFORNIA CLASSICS

CALIFORNIA CLASSICS

COLIN BURNHAM

Osprey Colour Series

Published in 1990 by Osprey Publishing Limited
59 Grosvenor Street
London W1X 9DA

British Library Cataloguing in Publication Data
Burnham, Colin
California classics
1. Cars. Convertible. American. History
I. Title
629.2'222

ISBN 0-85045-878-1

Printed in Hong Kong
Editor Nicholas Collins
Designer Angela Posen

For my son, Jack, with love.

About the author

Colin Burnham is an English freelance photographer and journalist who has specialized in American orientated automotive subjects for more than ten years. His interest in Americana dates back to the early sixties when, as a child, he was enamoured with a candy apple red Corvette given to him by his parents – matchbox size, that is. Formerly technical editor then features editor of *Street Machine* magazine, his work has appeared in numerous publications in Britain, Europe and the US, and this is his third book in the Osprey Colour Series, following *Air-cooled Volkswagens* and *Classic Volkswagens*. He lives in West London and drives a 1971 Rover 3.5 Coupé.

Acknowledgments

The author would like to thank *National Car Rental* and all its staff at LAX for making this book possible, Tony Thacker at *Osprey* for giving it the go-ahead, *Pan-Am* for an experience you can't beat, *Kodak* for their superb quality Kodachrome 64, the editors of the *Standard Catalog of American Cars (1946–75)* for chronicling all the hard-core facts and figures pertaining to the cars pictured, likewise the auto/social historians whose books and articles provided a wealth of information; *Dream Cars* of Battersea, South London, importers of classic American cars, for demonstrating their interest; Clive Househam, *Street Machine* Editor, for being an all-round good guy, and Ange for her help and encouragement throughout the project.

Back cover

Gimme the moonlight, gimme the Pontiac and leave the rest to me . . .?

Title page

National Car Rental's impressive billboard at Los Angeles airport entices passengers arriving from all walks of life to sample one of their California Classics; a genuine 'California Experience' if ever there was one

Previous spread

Choose your 'Classic' and cruise down Memory Lane . . .

Europcar National

The convertibles pictured are available for rent from National Car Rental at LAX at the time of writing, along with around ninety others. More information is available direct from National Car Rental, 9419 Airport Blvd., Los Angeles, CA 90045, USA. Tel: (213) 670 4950; or through National's European subsidiary, Europcar.

CONTENTS

1955 Cadillac Eldorado: one of the finest convertibles in National Car Rental's 'California Classics' collection

INTRODUCTION

California Classics is the collective name given by National Car Rental to an impressive collection of 1950s and early 1960s American convertibles which are available for rent at Los Angeles International Airport (LAX).

Instigated on the crest of the seemingly never-breaking waves of nostalgia for the fabulous fifties, National's idea, launched in the autumn of 1987, was not so much a commercial gamble as a creative attempt to achieve recognition within one of the most competitive marketplaces in the Southern California 'autopolis'. And no doubt the resultant publicity has achieved just that. Moreover, the Classics have proved so popular that most of the 120-or-so cars which comprise the fleet rarely get the chance to cool down. Probably the largest single collection of classic convertibles in the United States, they represent an investment of some $3 million.

Los Angeles has intrigued me since my first visit in 1984. Fashioned out of a desert on the edge of an ocean, *Elay* has become a fragmented collection of paradoxical communities and individualistic lifestyles, desired and despised, second in population to the New York metropolitan area and expected to exceed it by the year 2000. It was once the destination of the greatest migration in history and is now the nation's prime port of entry for new immigrants. It is not a melting pot or stew, but, given the climate, more a gazpacho of people and ideas.

The vitality which has formed LA is all round, in radiant technicolour; brilliant blue skies, gorgeous golden sunshine, shocking pink houses, pastel storefronts, incandescent coloured billboards, and vehicles of every hue. In a plane descending into LAX, I reminded myself, the City of Angels has also produced smog, crime, crowded freeways and other urban ills, as well as economic disparities and social and racial tension. But jump back, Jack. That's not what was on my mind at the luggage claim area in November 1987 . . .

I needed to rent a car, one of those sterile, anonymous 'same old cars'. The cheapest available. At the time it didn't matter which company I rented from, but, in retrospect, I am very grateful to the National counter clerk who offered me the most favourable deal on a Toyota something-or-other.

As the courtesy bus entered National's lot a wink of chrome caught my eye and – *Holy Fins!* There were fifties cars everywhere, or so it seemed. All convertibles, too. The bus driver told me that the 'Classics' were a recent addition and, providing I was a member of National's Emerald Club ($50 a year subscription), I could rent one for *fordy-nine-ninedy-five* a day, plus mileage. The seeds were sown for the book you are now holding.

Back in London ten days later, I called Tony Thacker (then Osprey's commissioning editor) straight away. TT was keen – so keen, in fact, that within a month he was out in Tinsel Town sampling a 1956 Chevy convertible, having sealed the book deal at National's headquarters in Minneapolis. The company would allow me to use their California Classics for photographic purposes, on the basis that the car in question wasn't already booked out. The prospect seemed almost too good to be true; the experience itself was even better.

My companion and I spent almost a month cruising around LA in the 'cool' convertibles pictured on these pages – thirty-three of them in all. Everything from a gaudy, gargantuan 1959 Cadillac to a quirky little Metropolitan; everywhere from Surf City to the Mojave Desert. A million miles from the grey UK of November to be sure. I sometimes wonder, now, whether it was all just a dream, a good escapist movie; a metaphor for Los Angeles itself.

In a city where status and style are measured largely by what you drive, our wheels made a none-too-subtle statement: 'Hey, look at me. Aren't I a lot of fun?'. Everywhere we drove, people waved, smiled, made complimentary remarks and offers to buy, and told us how they used to have one just like it. The cars were ostentatious reminders of a happier, more innocently optimistic time. A unique period in which the frank acknowledgement of a robust consumer appetite made the design of such extravagant cars possible. It was, undoubtedly, the high point in America's love affair with the automobile, and the convertibles pictured herein must surely represent the ultimate in Motown glamour.

I loved them, if only for their brazen vulgarity in this so-called 'designer' age. Not to mention their 'period living room' comfort, and the feeling of freedom once you were ensconsed behind their giant steering wheels on the freeway. In a fifties 'land yacht' you are not tied-in like you're piloting a closed-cockpit airplane. Indeed, the Standard American Driving Position – left arm hanging out the window, right steering – feels wholly natural, even to a Limey.

When you look under the bonnet you can actually see the spark plugs, eight of them, as opposed to vacuum hoses, micro chips and widgets all over the place. And the ride – so soft and smooth, not that short, choppy ride that is the hallmark of every modern-day performance car. Naturally, the two-ton dinosaurs wallowed and squeeled around corners in the best Bmovie tradition, and the effortless power of an old V8 with auto transmission that enables you to kick-down and rumble past the small fry leaves absolutely no doubt that you are driving a *real* American car. Similarly, power-assisted everything and the view front and rear, across acres of enamelled sheetmetal. I wasn't especially wild about their manoeuverability in certain locations, however, but that quintessentially California experience of 'cruising along the Pacific Coast Highway with the wind in your hair' will stay logged in my mind *forever* . . .

Many of the would-be free spirits who choose to rent a California Classic are businessmen in the 40-to-50 age group. They were the kids of the family in the days when Madison Avenue copywriters were reminding Mom and Dad to bless DeSoto for making seats that let you step out like a lady; Chevy chic; Pontiac's upholstery with the off-the-shoulder look; Dodge, with the magic touch of tomorrow; and dramatic Edsel styling that was here to stay.

These now-responsible citizens may never have had the chance to drive their teenage dream cars before, but at fifty tax-deductible dollars a day, they're not slow to seize the opportunity now. In fact, National sometimes gets repeated requests for the same car from businessmen who wish to impress clients. Likewise from back-street guys dating up-town girls.

Of course, tourists love the way the old rag-tops fit the laid-back image associated with LA, while residents often rent them for special occasions. One of the stories I heard concerned a wealthy attorney who rented a 1956 Ford to celebrate a twenty-fifth wedding anniversary by re-creating, right down to the last details, the couple's very first date. *Only in California* . . .

National acquires most of its convertibles from auctions in the 'dry' states. For the most part, they are in 'medium' condition, since 'high-point' restorations would obviously lose too much of their value too quickly in the rental business. The company is constantly adding to the collection as well as selling off cars – often to clients who just *had* to take them home.

Every *MRLD* (Emerald Club) car is overhauled as necessary and equipped with seat belts front and rear, an alternator in place of the original generator, and other such concessions to latter-day technology. A mileage log followed by a check-over after each rental, along with regular preventative maintenance performed by a specially selected team of mechanics, lessens the likelihood of a mechanical failure – such that the chances are said to be only marginal higher than with a normal rental car. It's a well-oiled system, and as if to prove it, *pitchaman* (as I came to be known) was trailered back to base just once during the entire month.

Had it been feasible, I would have loved to stay longer and photograph *all* the California Classics. Hopefully though, the cross-section pictured on these pages will give you a good idea of the sort of cars that would have been commonplace on Main Street, California more than a quarter of a century ago. If you enjoy this book half as much as I've enjoyed putting it together, you will ease my sense of conscience considerably. It wasn't all fun and games, *honest*!

Colin Burnham
London, England, 1989

David Allsop from New York, resident painter at my hotel for the duration of the assignment, was particularly impressed with the red 1957 Chevy. But then he would have loved to have driven home in the 1950 Pontiac, the 1955 T-Bird, the 1957 Vette, the 1961 Impala – in fact any of the 33 cars I had the good fortune to sample

HAPPY DAYS

January 1, 1950: Harry 'Give 'em Hell' Truman is President of the United States, and the nation has had almost five years to re-align itself following the Armageddon that World War 2 promised and nearly delivered. The pendulum that swung almost to breaking point in one direction is now swinging the other way; a new world is rising, built on the ashes of innocence. Those whose nature and job it is to worry still have communism, the atom bomb and the cold war to occupy their minds, but to most Americans, *en route* to the planet of Plenty, such concerns seem somehow distant. It is time to be happy, to live on the never-never, and the exuberant inclination to throw out the old and dance into the future manifests itself in every aspect of American culture.

1950 Pontiac Chieftain: *in the post-war years, the faces of American cars tended towards hostility and defensiveness, such that in some cases one is tempted to find the countenance of Senator Joseph McCarthy glaring out from the front end. Compared to a 1950 Buick, the Silver Streak straight 8 is almost 'plain Jane', but the car had plenty of power by the standards of its day*

Above
Ever since its introduction as one of the four original makes of General Motors in 1926, Pontiac's basic premise for success was to give the Pontiac owner much of the luxury, comfort and fine detail of expensive cars at a price just higher than the lower-priced lines. Forty years ago, this classic convertible cost $2,190. Today, you'd pay around five times that figure for a top-notch example

The automobile, perhaps more than anything else, symbolized the freedom which the allies fought so hard to retain. New cars had been in painfully short supply in the immediate post-war years, but 1950 saw deliveries quadruple to a staggering 6½ million vehicles, most of which were bigger and better than ever before. A construction and employment boom had put more people to work at better wages than at any other time in history, and a new car was considered an essential constituent of the American Dream, much like the washing machine, the TV set and the backyard barbecue. It was the dawning of a new decade in which middle class Moms would bake their collective apple pie in new, spacious suburban homes with wall-to-wall carpeting and all mod cons, and drive 'futuramic' cars with 'dynamic-aero' styling, powerful V8 engines and smooth automatic transmission. *Autopia* was just around the corner . . .

The seductive shapes of war-time machinery influenced the approach of every automotive designer in De-

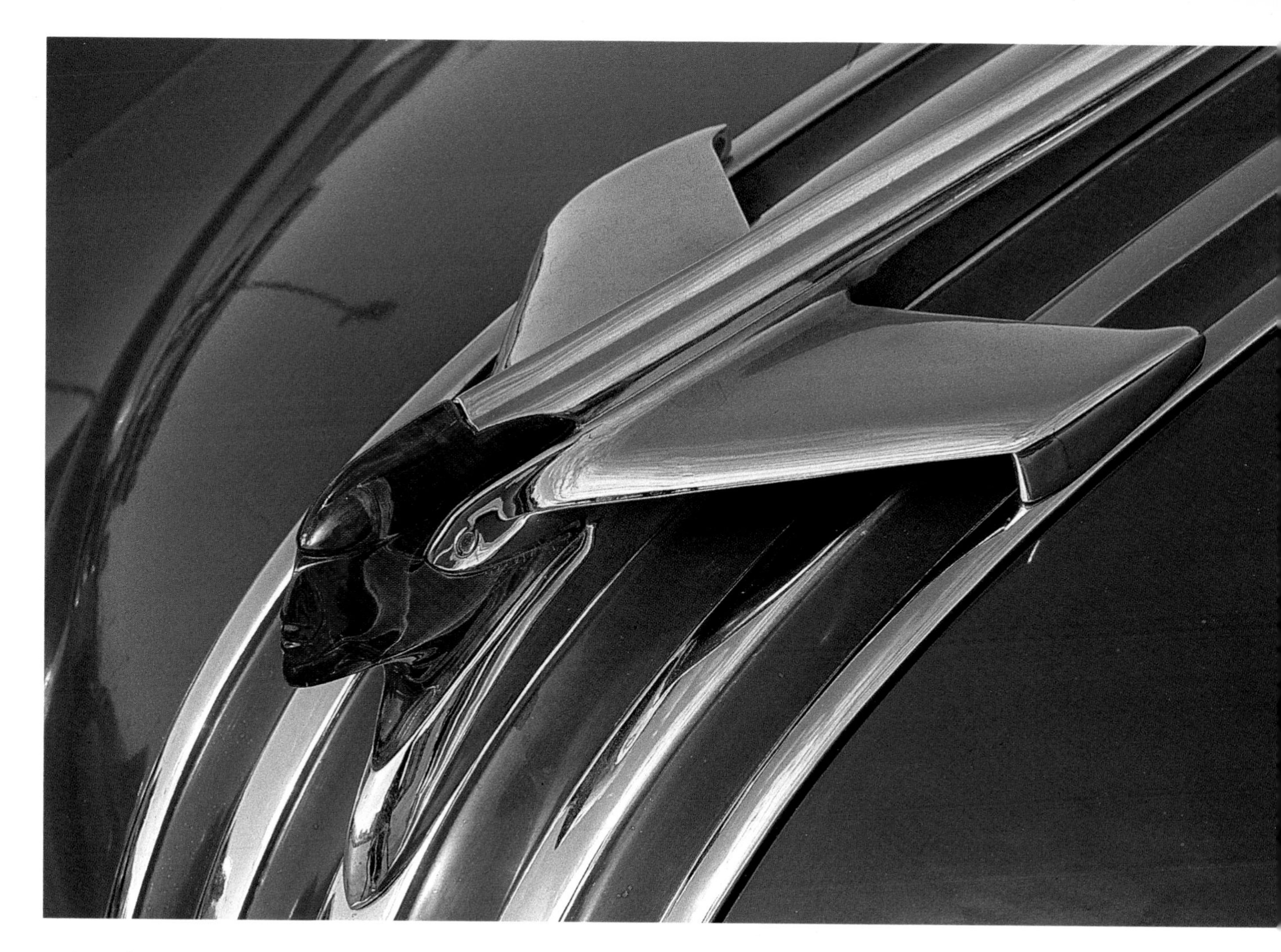

troit, and none more so than Harley Earl, General Motors' chief stylist. Earl, now revered as the grandfather of US auto design, linked car styling to the aeroplane look as early as the first Cadillac tail-fin in 1948, and it was he who catalyzed the aesthetic revolution that swept through the industry in the 1950s. Nuances of aeronautical and aerospace motifs appeared gradually through the early part of the decade, and by the time the Russians launched Sputnik in 1957, the American public was thoroughly acquainted with the

Above
The traditional 'Indianhead' adorned Pontiac hoods until 1957, likewise the characteristic 'Silver Streak' chrome strips that appeared both on the hood and rear deck. Silver Streak styling was originated in 1935 by Virgil Exner, a young designer who went on to achieve fame and recognition at Chrysler in the late fifties

Overleaf
The mountains above Palm Springs – where the rich play and the rest play rich – provide the setting for this view of the sleek 'Streak. The traditional rural mailbox, designed in 1915, represents another classic American artefact

PINON DR
MFD. BY
JACKES-EVANS
MFG. CO.

FULTON CORPORATION
FULTON, ILLINOIS
FULTON CORPORATION
FULTON, ILLINOIS

Above
*Hood decoration, **1952 Oldsmobile Ninety-Eight**. Oldsmobile has the longest historical trail of any existing American manufacturer, and in the early fifties their ohv Rocket V8-engined cars were virtually unbeatable on the budding NASCAR stock car racing circuit – not to mention the street, where they were used by the California Highway Patrol*

symbolic emblems of space travel. By the end of the era, every manufacturer was building cars that looked like fighter planes and rocket ships equipped with four wheels and dripping with chrome. The Space Race was on, at ground level.

American cars of this period, especially convertibles, offered performance, excitement, stylish good looks and 'the power to turn a wish into motion'. The undeclared horsepower race was underway as early as 1949, when GM introduced a 160 bhp overhead-valve V8 in their Cadillac and Oldsmobile ranges. Chrysler led the pack in 1951, though by the time Dwight D. Eisenhower ascended to the Presidency in 1953, the prestigious Cadillac's power output had been raised to 210 hp, with luxury car rivals Lincoln just five horses behind. And so it went. That is, until 1955, when Chevrolet followed Ford's example and introduced their first ohv V8. The celebrated 'small block' Chevy engine was lighter, more compact and produced more power per pound/cubic inch than any other V8 on the market. It was wrapped in an elegant new package, and it shifted the balance of power

Right
***1953 Lincoln Capri**, a car named after a town in the Bay of Naples and pictured at the Queen Mary/Spruce Goose complex in Long Beach harbour. The trans-Atlantic luxury liner was acquired by the city of Long Beach in 1967 and has since served as a hotel-cum-tourist attraction. Visitors can walk the length of the ship – the equivalent of three American football fields – then proceed to marvel at the sight of Howard Hughes' giant prototype 'flying boat', the Spruce Goose, which was designed to transport troops and equipment to Europe during World War 2*

Overleaf
In 1950, Lincoln was recognised as the limousine builder by appointment to the White House, but most Americans who could afford a luxury car preferred to vote Cadillac. Thus Earl S. MacPherson, president of Ford's Lincoln-Mercury division, enforced changes in strategy that resulted in the all-new Lincoln Capri for 1952. The car had sharp, contemporary styling with re-designed ball-joint front suspension and, moreover, a new 317 cid ohv V8 which produced an impressive 0.64 bhp per cubic inch – 0.01 bhp more than a Cadillac. During its three-year production run, the Capri gained three successive victories in its class in the punishing Carrera Panamericana Road Race across Mexico, an achievement which firmly established Lincoln's reputation as a manufacturer of 'hot' cars

CALIFORNIA
MRLD 27

Above
Power steering, power brakes, power windows and a 4-way power seat were all standard issue in the top-of-the-range 1952–54 Lincoln convertible, nevertheless Cadillac still sold more than four times as many ragtops during this period

Right
National's California Classics attract attention wherever they are driven, particularly the 'Milestone' cars as certified by the Milestone Car Society of America. This enterprising Japanese photographer stepped in on the shoot and has probably been well rewarded by now for his efforts . . .

between heavyweight prestige cars and their lesser relatives. Suddenly, Everyman's Chevy, Ford or Plymouth had the kind of power that would have been unimaginable in the forties, a time when marketing values stressed virtuous reliability, sound engineering and sensible styling. Cars of the fifties were built to gratify the ego and satisfy that fundamental American desire for travel for its own sake. In *style*. Driving, whether going somewhere or 'just cruising', became a national pastime.

A product of the expanding consumer society was the new concept of the teenager or youth market, as symbolized by teen idols James Dean and Elvis Presley, and exported throughout the Western hemisphere. For a generation with more freedom and money than ever before, being able to drive was a matter of social life or death. Whether a so-called hood who spent his time racing up and down Main Street in a hot rod, or a clean-cut nice guy who took Babs to the sock

QUEEN MARY
EMERALD
SEP CALIFORNIA
MRLD 27

1954 Hudson Metropolitan: *Why, you may wonder, would anyone wish to rent this over-sized dodgem car when they could cruise around in a 1959 Caddy for the same price? Indeed, that's a mystery, but what's more intriguing is why such a car ever went on sale in the US in the first place. The Metropolitan story can be traced back to 1950, when the Nash-Kelvinator Corporation displayed their humble prototype at the Waldorf Astoria Hotel in New York. The passing public were handed questionnaires headed 'Does America want the Economy Car?', and were given a choice of engines: a Fiat 500 unit offering 18 bhp and 45 mpg for $950, or an engine of double the size (Fiat or Triumph) which would propel the steel jelly-mould to 70 mph, return 35 mpg and add $50 to the price. Not surprisingly, those curious parties who spared the time voted 3-to-1 in favour of the larger engine. This kind of market research led to the production contract being awarded to the Austin Motor Company of Longbridge, England, and by 1957 (the year Austin began manufacturing right-hand drive versions for the UK market) more than 30,000 Austin A40-engined Metropolitans had been shipped across the Atlantic. The car was an anachronism, for certain, but a further 60,000 units consolidated its presence, nipping between the lumbering land yachts of the late fifties, before production ceased in mid-1960. But that still doesn't explain why the car pictured here is a 'Hudson', when the model is commonly referred to as a 'Nash' or 'Met'. That's no mystery. Shortly after production began, Nash merged with Hudson to form AMC and whilst the two operations were being integrated, some of the cars were badged 'Hudson' so they could be sold through existing Hudson dealerships. While the Cove Motel on the PCH may be a long way from the Waldorf, the little Nash – sorry, 'Hudson' Metropolitan lives on . . .*

10
CALIFORNIA

'Austin of England are proud to announce that the new Nash Metropolitan sedan and convertible, now announced by the Nash-Kelvinator Corporation of Detroit for sale in the USA and Canada, is being produced at Longbridge using material of entirely British manufacture and basic design. This car promises to become one of the the country's greatest dollar-earners and is a glowing tribute to the versatility of Britain's motor industry.' (1954 advertisement headed 'Britain's Newest Dollar Earner')

Right
Exterior arm rests reinforce the fact that this car, though built and sold in Britain, was designed by Americans for Americans

hop in Dad's convertible, a teenager's life in the fifties was lived in and with the car. Being 'grounded' or without wheels became the severest form of parental punishment. And any teenager in mid-fifties suburbia who couldn't drive was automatically labelled 'nerd'.

Disneyland opened in 1955, as did the first McDonald's. Like the Holiday Inn chain of motels that proliferated in 1951, it offered 'no surprises'. It was clean, fast and convenient, and for a nation infatuated with the automobile, it was fun. What better place for a burger and a chocolate malt than in your new Chevy convertible? Roadside establishments serving the needs of the motorist for food, accommodation and amusement sprang up like mushrooms, and the 'drive-in' variety exemplified the new 'don't walk, ride' America. There were

Left

In the year that Roger Bannister ran the first 4-minute mile in England, The Autocar *recorded a top speed of 74 mph for the 42 hp 1200 cc 1954 Metropolitan. The magazine liked the car and thought it would be ideal for 'running people to the station, taking the children to school and shopping'. Thirty-five years later, this rare example, with its custom-made spare wheel cover, provides a source of amusement for all who see it tootling along the Pacific coastal roads*

drive-in cinemas, drive-in liquor stores, banks, laundries – California even provided the drive-in funeral parlour where the motorist could say his prayers without leaving the security of his car.

When Charles E. Wilson, president of General Motors, made the statement, 'What's good for the country is good for General Motors' in 1953, it was both an observation and a prediction. The automobile was good for America in the early fifties, and with its growing appetite for glamour, power and fantasy, there seemed to be no limit to the role it was destined to play. ■

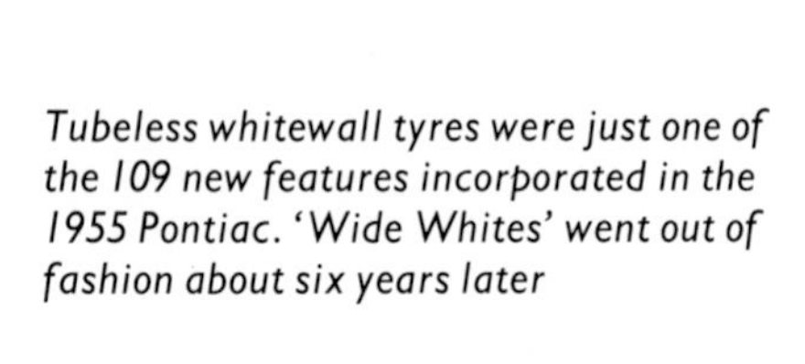

Tubeless whitewall tyres were just one of the 109 new features incorporated in the 1955 Pontiac. 'Wide Whites' went out of fashion about six years later

PONTIAC

Above
1955 Pontiac Star Chief, *framed by the spectacular restaurant-in-the-sky at Los Angeles International Airport (LAX). During the fifties, Pontiac built some sturdy cars, some pretty cars and, like most other auto makers, some garish cars. But only a few had the combination of glitter, horsepower and eye appeal that made them 'dream cars' when they arrived on the showroom floor. This is one of them*

Below

Accompanying the all-new $17\frac{1}{2}$ft long body Pontiac's first modern overhead-valve V8, known as the Strato Streak. With an initial displacement of 287 cubic inches and a power rating of 200 bhp with a four-barrel carb, it was of strong, conventional design and ran on regular gas. It came with a standard 'three-on-the-tree' manual gearbox or optional four-speed Hydramatic drive. The three star emblem on the front fenders and doors was one of the Star Chief's distinguishing features

In 1955, Ford added a new model to its line – not just any new model, but an entirely new type of car. Up until then, there had been sedans, coupes, station wagons and, in 1953, Chevrolet's somewhat spartan, six-cylinder Corvette sports car. But the ***1955 Ford Thunderbird*** *was being called something else: a 'personal' luxury car. Combining the appearance of a sports car with the power and driveability of a luxury coupé, the two-seater T-Bird captured the hearts of Americans in a special way and has since become an icon of American popular culture. It was graceful and well-balanced in an era ruled by extravagance and excess, and with a big V8 it outsold the fibreglass-bodied Corvette by 5:1 during its three-year production run. Luxury and prestige with a sporty image; the Thunderbird was a statement of what most Americans wanted their lives to be*

Above
Exhaust outlets were incorporated in each of the 1955 T-Bird's rear overriders which gave the car a distinctive roar; a subtle gesture to the jet-age styling of the period

FINS & FANTASY

One can view the latter half of the fifties as the Golden Age of automotive styling. The cars that poured off the Motown assembly lines were the stuff of dreams, exhibiting variety and verve in their design which reflected the national exuberance of the period. They became longer, lower, wider and more powerful each year, as Harley Earl and his fellow stylists interpreted their fantasies into chrome and sculptured steel. The automobile was America's key product, and from 1955 onwards it occupied an even larger place in the consumers' consciousness – not to mention their garages – than ever before.

Most of the manufacturers had been in a cycle of major change every three years, with face-lifts in between, whereby 'newness' appeared on the American car in steady increments. This gradualism speeded-up

The shape of fins to come (sic) was first seen on the ***1955 Cadillac Eldorado Special Sport Convertible****, otherwise known as the 'Biarritz'. The rest of the line continued to use the shaved-down tail fin design that had been a Cadillac hallmark since 1948. Note the round, jet-style exhaust outlets at each end of the bumper*

Above

California gleaming: the Eldorado – literally 'a golden land' – pictured against a backdrop of palms at Playa Del Ray. When this California Classic rolled off the line, Elvis Presley was a fast-rising star of a new form of pop music that would launch an undeclared war between a large segment of American parents and their teenagers, many of whom had money as well as ambition and showed remarkably little reticence about either. As Billboard *introduced their first Top 100 chart, the automakers of Detroit saw the new tide of adult affluence coming and capped their regular lines with what one magazine defined as 'a class of super-luxury cars neglected since the 1930s'. These were the Packhard Caribbean, the Chrysler Imperial, the Lincoln Continental Mk II and the epitome of automotive elegance, the Cadillac Eldorado. But while the competition may have been fierce, Cadillac was never really threatened as 'the' standard of the prestige car world. The company achieved record sales of around 140,000 in 1955 (3,950 of which were Biarritz convertibles) as the industry as a whole reached its all-time peak*

Above
GM introduced bullet-shaped protruberances above the front bumpers on its Cadillacs in 1953. These symbolic pieces of chrome came to be known as 'Dagmars', in honour of a well-endowed, none-too-bright blonde bombshell of late-night TV. Cadillacs featured them for a decade and several other makes adopted them as well. They were laughed at, but they raised sales

halfway through the decade, as many models were completely re-vamped every two years, and in some cases annually. The face-lifts became more noticeable, too. While the need to produce a range of cars that appeared to be totally new every year often led designers to great flights of imagination, it also encouraged them to be arbitrary – which was the main reason why the public so eagerly awaited the arrival of the new model. This sales philosophy was known as 'planned obsolescence', and it worked for the manufacturers because they were riding the tide of a seller's market.

Detroit produced more cars in 1955 than at any other time this century – more than $65 billion worth, or 20 per cent of the gross national product. That was the year in which Sloan Wilson, in *The Man in the Grey Flannel Suit*, wrote: 'We might as well admit that what we want is a big house and a new car and trips to Florida in the winter, and plenty of life assurance. When you come right down to it, a man has no damned right to say that money doesn't matter.' A few years later, a Ford executive reiterated this view of 1950s American society when he said, 'Volkswagens were bought not by those who needed cheap transportation, but by grey-flannelled non-conformists.' This was an era of solid patriotism and 'buy American', and, for the most part, Ford's spokesman was probably right.

Nothing could be more detrimental to one's social status than being caught in yesterday's car; you were what you drove, and the bigger the better. Each year the conscientious consumer 'moved up' to a new car and, in some cases, to the *ne plus ultra* of cars, the convertible. 'Flop tops' were fun, flashy and fast, and their innate sense of freedom and glamour appealed to many more Americans than was ever reflected in sales figures. No matter that you were only driving to the grocery store to pick up a quart of milk, the topless car made it seem like you were bound on some exciting rendezvous. 'Motivational research' showed that although the majority of men bought sedans, they were more attracted to convertibles. In the same way as a man might have a fling with a glamorous woman but marry the practical one, psychologists deduced, so he might want the rag-top but end up buying the sedan.

Right
This 1955 Eldorado was originally owned by legendary TV Newsman, Chet Huntley. He would have paid around $6,300 for the car, and probably waxed lyrical about its 270 horsepower engine (not to mention its nifty but now missing fibreglass tonneau cover) after taking delivery. 1955 marked Cadillac's 41st consecutive year of V8 availability

Below
Along with all the usual Cadillac refinements, the Eldorado came with a rather novel 'Autronic Eye', a device that detected the headlights of oncoming vehicles and dipped the Caddy's accordingly. This was a car for the man with more important things on his mind

Left
The annual beauty treatment for the ***1956 Cadillac*** *included a closer-knit version of the distinctive egg-crate grille, along with a script positioned on the left side. Styling motifs developed by General Motors, in particular, spread a certain image of the USA all around the globe*

***1956 Thunderbird**, Cafe 50s, Lincoln Boulevard, Venice: a great place to stop for a burger, fries and a real chocolate malt. There are over a dozen authentic fifties-style diners included on National's 'Cruise Down Memory Lane' map, some of which have appeared on sites that only a decade or so earlier had been cleared of similar establishments in the name of progress*

SERVICE
50's
OPEN
We win more awards

Above
Collectors generally consider the 1956 T-Bird – distinguished by a Continental (spare wheel) Kit – to be the cream of the crop. The 1957 edition, which sold around 21,000 and was offered with a 340 bhp supercharged mill, sported a combined bumper/grille and modest tail fins. Back in the fifties, Ford's styling chief, George Walker (an ex-dress designer known as 'the Cellini of Chrome'), was quoted as saying: 'The ultimate in elegance is to be dressed in a white suit, driving a white Thunderbird with white upholstery, with a white Afghan hound beside you.' Not everyone shared his definition of American chic

What evolved from this research was the pillarless hard top. With its wide-open convertible look, it supposedly represented a union of wife and mistress, and it became *the* bodystyle of the 1950s.

One of the great national projects during the Eisenhower years was the construction of a network of interstate highways; 41,000 miles of unlimited horizons linking every state in the Union. It was made possible by the Highway Trust Fund,

Right
1956 Ford Fairlane Sunliner *– where else but The Golden State? Cadillacs and Lincolns were the cars people saw as symbols of success on TV and the silver screen, but Chevrolets, Fords and Plymouths were the cars that Everyman drove. Moreover, in 1956, only one out of every 25 Ford buyers could stretch to a rag-top. Ironically perhaps, the seven-model Fairlane series was named after Henry Ford's mansion in Dearborn, Michigan*

a multi-billion dollar account made up of car and 30 cents-a-gallon gasoline taxes which enabled the Federal Government to foot 90 per cent of the bill. And the more roads Uncle Sam built, the more cars he produced.

By 1956, Madison Avenue was advocating that two was better than one, and that two cars weren't a luxury, they were a necessity for the modern, suburban family in which Mom did most of the chauffeuring. The manufacturers realised what dealers had known all along: a car had to appeal to the wife as well as the husband. Ads offered women the opportunity to be 'Chevy chic' and to match Pontiac's 'off-the-shoulder look' interior to their own fashion ensembles. The DeSoto with wide doors was said to be 'wonderful for party dresses and tight skirts', and there was Dodge's infamous LeFemme, a special model in pink and charcoal grey with matching umbrella and purse rack as standard equipment. One lady journalist, writing in the *New York Journal*, noted: 'These days you can have as much fun shopping for a car as you do shopping for a dress or living room curtains . . .'

Left
'Sunliner' was the name given to the convertible Fairlane, for reasons that don't have to be explained when you rent one in sunny SoCal

Right
Redondo Beach palm trees reflect on the hood. Beneath it was not the original 272 cubic inch V8, I'm sure, but something much more potent. This thing really hauled!

Below right
With the late afternoon sun on its side, the two-tone Ford exhibits a rakish look of motion, enhanced by the chrome side sweep mouldings featuring simulated exhaust outlets at the tail end. Note the actual exhaust outlets at either end of the bumper

Every model in each manufacturer's range vied for first place in styling, performance and glamour. Though the General's Cadillac had featured modest tail fins since 1948, the big leap into outer space began in 1955 with the Cadillac Eldorado and a new range of cars from Chrysler Corporation styled by Virgil Exner, former understudy to Harley Earl at GM. They featured acute angles, plains and horizontal edges instead of traditional rounded curves, with sweeping tail fins for the '100 million dollar look' Chrysler and DeSoto. The makers described their up-swept rear ends as 'feminine', while experts on the subconscious thought they were 'invitations to copulate'. At General Motors, the feeling was that tail fins gave definition to the rear of the car for the first time; they made the back as interesting as the front. The Cadillac's fins – reputedly derived

Fairlane
1MRLD93

Chevrolet

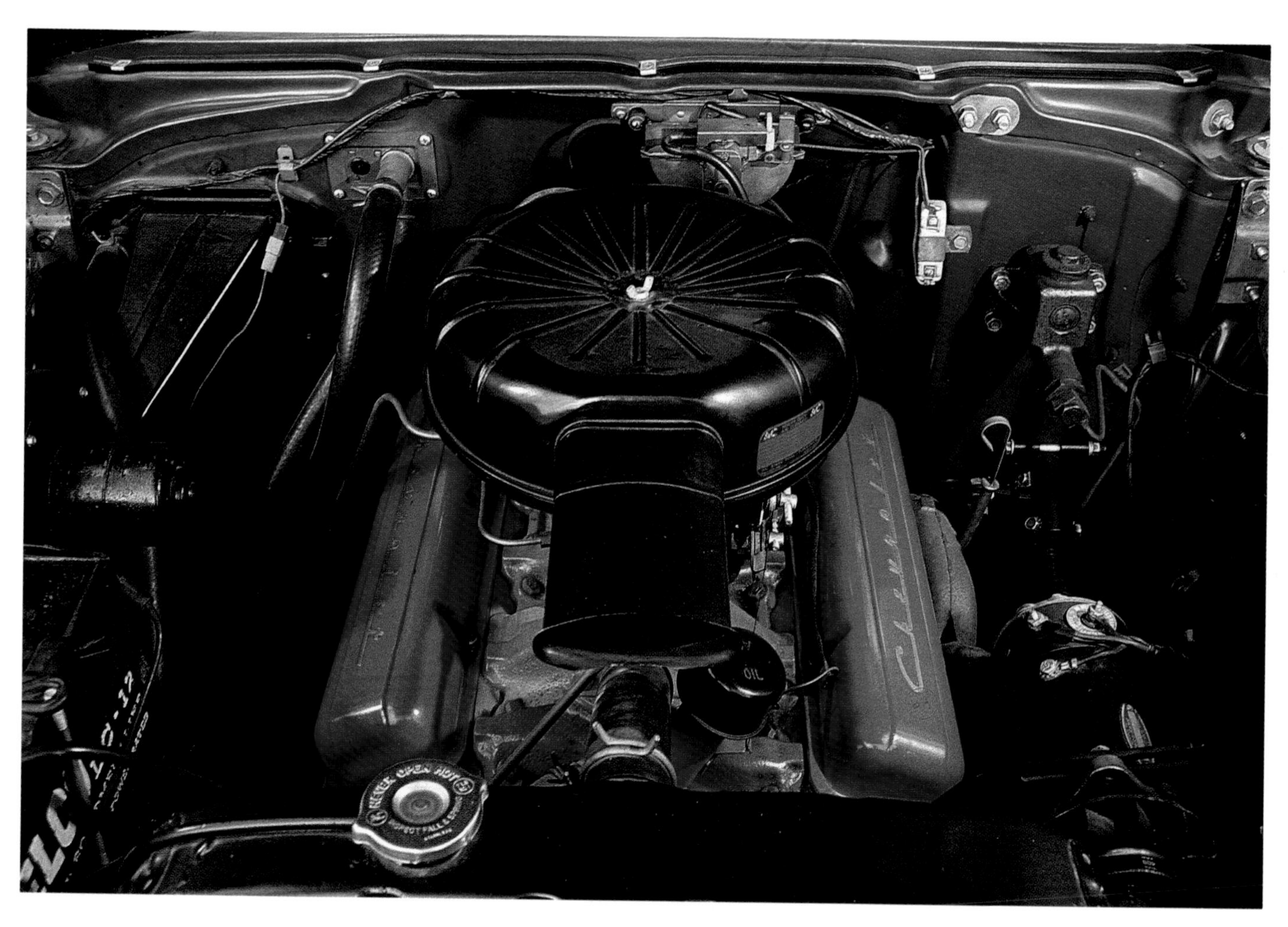

1957 Chevrolet Bel Air: *the classic 1950s Chevy. With the introduction of the legendary small-block Chevrolet V8 and a new body style in 1955, GM's economy division offered glamour and power in the same proportion as luxury cars did – at a far lower cost. Though the levels of luxury and styling indulgence were somewhat less marked, the performance distinction vanished altogether. Chevy's first-ever V8 was an engineering triumph. From its 265 cubic inch/162 bhp inauguration, it became the first fuel-injected V8 to produce one horsepower-per-cubic inch in 1957 (or so Chevrolet claimed). Road & Track had already said that the 225 hp 1956 Chevy could out-accelerate any production car in the United States, so when the 1957 came along with the optional 283 bhp motor it had to be a sure-fire winner, bearing in mind that the great horsepower race was in full swing. Unfortunately, Chevrolet, like all of General Motors, was also in the grip of the styling change frenzy encouraged by Harley Earl, who was apparently unwilling to let a good thing be. The 1957 was essentially a beautifully re-styled version of the 1956 and 1955 models, but it was replaced by an all-new car for 1958 – which, in turn, was replaced by the brand new 1959 Chevrolet. This practice, known as 'dynamic obsolescence', abated in 1960, but sadly the brakes went on much too late to prevent Chevrolet's most eloquent styling from being swept out by garish overstatement*

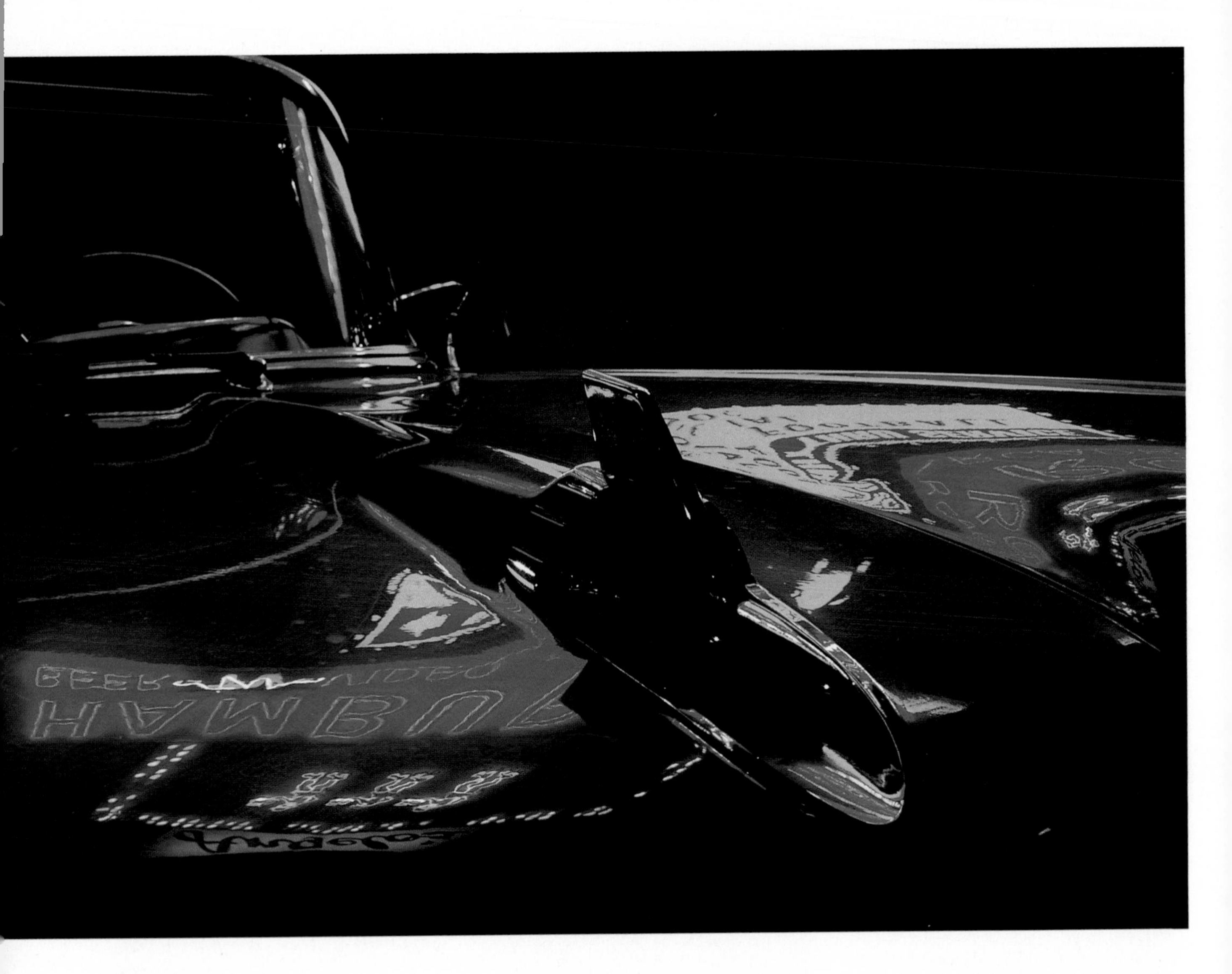

Above
'Windsplit' bulges running along both sides of the hood were decorated with 'bomb sight' ornaments . . . but is it 'art'?

from the twin-tailed Lockheed P-38 fighter plane – were fast becoming contagious, and by 1956 if your car didn't have them you could buy a tack-on set for most models for around $35.

In 1950s American parlance, anything wonderful was called 'dreamy'. A handsome guy was a 'dreamboat', a girl 'dreambait', and the most wonderful car imaginable was a 'dream car'. Most manufacturers had at least one dream car – but they weren't available in the showrooms. The term was generally applied to what were essentially styling exercises, three-dimensional visions of the future; vehicles to tantalize the car-crazy public at major auto shows around the coun-

try. They were loaded with gizmos and looked truly out of this world. Many of their features later appeared on production models. Others, like rear-mounted jet turbine engines and four-wheel front steering, were simply exorbitant ideas that would never happen – but they captured the public's imagination, nonetheless. The 'dream car' concept originated at General Motors before the war, and gained popularity after GM unveiled a line of futuristic prototypes at their glitzy *Motorama* show at the Waldorf Astoria in 1949. The Corvette was the only dream car to enter series production in a basically unaltered state, in 1953.

Above
Under the neon lights at Angelo's, *a well known hangout for hot rodders situated in Anaheim, the classic Chevy's classic two-tone interior*

OR • BEER
UNDRIES AND
$7.99
$8.99
$1.99
+ TX A SIX PACK
8OZ CANS

Another one of National's sought-after ***1957 Chevy Bel Air*** *rental cars, parked at a liquor store near Venice Beach. Chevrolet made just under 50,000 1957 convertibles and sold them at around $2,500 each. That means the model has increased in value by an average 30 per cent a year, based on today's prices*

Right
With its broad, flat fins there's no mistaking a 1957 Chevy, even when equipped with the now highly treasured Continental Kit

Below
Cruisin' the PCH (Pacific Coast Highway) between Malibu and Santa Monica. Are we having fun? You bet!

Above
Randy's Donuts *on Manchester Boulevard, Inglewood, provides the setting for National's* ***1957 Pontiac Star Chief****. 1957 marked the year in which two-toning switched from its previous half-a-car design to a sweep-spear along each flank. It was also the year in which Pontiac started producing the Bonneville ('America's Number I Road Car'), which gave the division a whole new performance image.* Randy's Donuts *is a classic example of 'Direct Programatic Architecture', an idea which evolved in the 1920s whereby the structure itself is the embodiment of what it is selling*

The great horsepower race which so delighted American youth really hotted up after Chevrolet introduced their new V8 models ('The Hot Ones') in 1955. The Big Three battled it out on the stock car racing circuit, the drag strip and the street, with engines that were producing phenomenal power compared to Ford's old flathead V8 and Chevrolet's 'Stovebolt' six. Chrysler's legendary 'hemi-head' V8 first appeared in 1955, and with 250 bhp on tap as standard, it equalled Cadillac's claim that year.

In 1956, the 331 cubic inch hemi was bored out to 354 and became the first Detroit V8 to produce one horsepower per cubic inch. Likewise in 1957, when *three ninety-two* was the displacement figure which made the high-performance Chrysler 300 the fastest, most powerful production car in America for the third year in a row. Meanwhile, the small block Chevy V8 grew from its original 265 cubic inches to 283 in 1957, 348 in 1958, 409 in 1961, and a whopping 427 cubic inches, or 7 litres, in 1967. And of course, Ford escalated their hot engine size just as rapidly. There was *no substitute for cubic inches . . .*

The wild, exciting cars of this period, with their hot engines and ice-cream sundae styling, could have

Left
The Pontiac's imposing front end embodies the unreality of 1950s America; a time when most Americans could afford to forget about the A-bomb and financial woes and go through life as if it were one big, open road leading toward a wonderful future . . . Under the hood is a 347 in version of Chevrolet's high performance V8

Above
Who could possibly resist the opportunity to go 'California dreamin'' in a 1957 Pontiac convertible? The chrome wand on the column selects the gears and adds to the fantasy

been aimed directly at the 'baby boomers'; the generation born during or directly after World War 2 with a taste for the 'new' and 'different'. As the older 'beat generation' portrayed in Jack Kerouac's 1957 novel *On the Road* embraced the progressive Jazz sounds of Dave Brubeck and Stan Kenton, American teenagers fell completely for the roughneck sensuality of Elvis Presley and other new Rock 'n Rollers like Chuck Berry, Little Richard and Jerry Lee Lewis. Adult America, meanwhile, continued its orgy of acquisition, but began to worry about the cultural ravages wrought by the aggressive new music and the rebellious teen heroes who were being projected onto drive-in screens all over the United States. The system was under threat . . . ■

Optional Continental kit makes this flashy fifties time-piece just inches short of 20 ft long. When a lever is pulled the 'donut' tips back a few degrees allowing the trunk lid to open

1957 Chevrolet Corvette: advance booking is certainly required to rent this California Classic. Back in 1953, when the Corvette made its debut, a 'Chevy', any Chevy, was considered the car that housewives drove to the supermarket to pick up peanut butter and jelly for their kids' lunch. Consequently most European sports car buffs snubbed the arrival of GM's new six-cylinder fibreglass two-seater, while those to whom it appealed simply couldn't afford it. Sales were positively miniscule at first, and had it not been for the arrival of the new Chevrolet V8 engine in 1955 followed by a face-lift in 1956, the Corvette would probably have died there and then. But it survives to this day albeit far removed from this truly classic 1957 model

Above
Sculptured front wings and doors were incorporated in 1956, along with conventional headlights in place of the original sloping type

Right
'Floating' tooth grille was a characteristic feature of all early Corvettes, 1953 through 1960

Left

With its European-style bucket seats, floor-mounted gearchange and lithe compact body, the Corvette was like no other American production car prior to the arrival of the Ford Thunderbird in 1955. A fuel-injected 1957 'Vette would accelerate from 0–60 in 5.8 seconds and reach 133 mph, though like most of the 6,339 examples produced that year, this 1957 came with the standard four-barrel 'two-eighty-three' (220 bhp). It did have a four-on-the-floor, however, and what a pleasure it was to shift . . .

'Duane' and his buddies gave this ***1957 Oldsmobile Golden Rocket Eighty-Eight*** *the A-OK at a motel in Garden Grove, Orange County. Oldsmobiles displayed the long, low, swoopy look of luxury and power throughout the fifties, and this one came from the factory with the famous J–2 Rocket engine. With three two-barrel carbs the J–2 reaped an honest 300 bhp from its 371 cubic inches*

The shape of the Olds' grille is echoed in the door panel treatment

Right
The Oldsmobile's characteristic 'gaping' grille was derived from the company's Starfire dream car of 1953. The term 'dream car' is believed to have been first penned in connection with General Motors' Motorama car shows of the early and mid-fifties. Harley Earl, head of GM Styling, used the Motorama shows to display stylists' ideas of America's future cars to the public. Virtually every manufacturer jumped onto the 'dream car' bandwagon, since public interest was so great

CALIFORNIA
MRLD 51

If fifties Americans ever found themselves bored by the new suburbs, there was always the possibility of hopping into the car and taking a drive. Increased car travel brought about thousands of roadside establishments, especially along the country's commercial strips. Fast-food restaurants, drive-in movies, bowling alleys, car washes, service stations and motels all vied with one another for the passing motorists' patronage. And would I like another drive in this 1957 Olds? Not many, Benny!

Right
If it's metal, chrome it!

Overleaf
1957 Mercury Monterey: Jack's Surfboards *at Huntington Beach – the cutting edge of California's surf scene ever since the days of the Beach Boys – seemed like a good backdrop for the Monterey, which was undoubtedly the least popular Classic in National's fleet. Not once did anybody choose to rent the car during my stay. The man largely responsible for the 1957 Mercury design said, years later, 'You could see how we could get the reputation as real hacks and chrome merchants, because looking at those cars, it would be hard to deny.' Amen*

PACIFIC
PCH
COAST HIGHWAY
SPORTSWEAR

AL OGATOR SAY'S, SURFS UP, GATOR DOWN
THE WATERPROOF

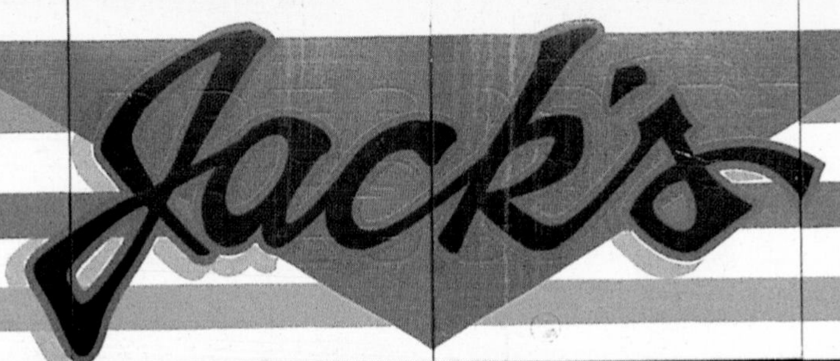
Jack's

ALEEDA
wetsuits

TOR
SPF 40
E PRODUCTS
WATERPROOF
8
HOURS
IN or OUT
of the
WATER
BODY GLOVE
OCEAN
PACIFIC
urfboards

LEEDA
wetsuits

Gregg Rippe, a real-life Californian surfer, liked the idea of having his picture taken for a book beside the Mercury. In 1957, On The Road *author Jack Kerouac declared, 'It is essential to dig the most for if you do not dig you lose your superiority over the square and so you are less likely to be cool'. Meanwhile, Pat Boone was top of the charts for 24 weeks with a schmaltzy song called 'Love Letters In The Sand'*

'Alan' has been selling flowers from a roadside stall near Marina Del Ray (LA's 'Riviera') for many years, and was flattered to be photographed with such a 'beautiful old car', a **1957 Ford Fairlane Sunliner**. Like the convertible Chevy, this was the working man's rag-top, representing the cheapest form of social status in a leisure-conscious climate. More than 77,000 found buyers in 1957. However, a mid-year addition to the Fairlane line-up, the Skyliner retractable hardtop (a convertible with a steel roof that slid into the trunk at the touch of a button), soon made the Sunliner something of a poor relation

Left

To help lower the car, thereby giving it a more streamlined look, Ford down-sized the wheels from 15 in to 14 in in 1957 and fitted them with some fancy finned covers. That was also the year in which Ford Division ousted Chevrolet from No. 1 position in the annual production race; one of only two occasions during the entire 1950s

Right

Heeeeerz Alan!

FEB
CALIFORNIA
MRLD

AMERICAN EXCESS

The three-speed automatic transmission in Chevrolet's 1958 Impala was described by its makers as 'revolutionary new, nothing-like-it Turboglide with triple-turbine take-off!' Which says a lot about the American auto industry as a whole as the fabulous fifties came to a close. This was Detroit's most baroque phase in which the ever greater elaboration of jet-age styling resulted in cars which, compared to those produced before or since, appear totally over-the-top. That non-functional mark of status, the tail fin, reached ridiculous proportions as it attempted to break free from the surrounding sheetmetal and ascend into the heavens. 'Chrome', as Bill Mitchell (Harley Earl's successor) said in retrospect, 'was layed on with a trowel'. And the big V8s were made even more powerful, if only to pull these land-yachts from their berths and power all their special features! These are the Yank tanks that provided travel by sofa in a convertible built for and easily exceeding 100 mph in cruise control . . .

*At 4,200 lbs kerbside, this chrome-encrusted **1958 Oldsmobile Dynamic Eighty-Eight** demanded more than was fair of its 265 tired-out horses. What a dinosaur!*

Above
Rarely would you find the streets beneath the imposing Westin Bonaventure Hotel as desolate as this, except on Thanksgiving Day. Downtown Los Angeles, with its modern skyscrapers, occupies only a tiny portion of the 464 square miles of urban sprawl they call Elay*. It's an octopus, with its body Downtown and its tentacles reaching out to Santa Barbara in the north, San Diego in the south and 60 miles inland to the mountain ranges of San Bernardino and San Jacinto*

Above
Armed like a medieval knight, this Bible-black behemoth exemplifies Detroit's obsession with tonnage and chrome in the late fifties. In essence, it's an exercise in pure form and visual semantics. Location: Downtown LA

Right
Shortly after the 1958 Olds was introduced, Ford stylist Alex Tremulis satirized the four chrome strips on the rear fenders by drawing in a clef and a few notes of music . . .

ARCO

CALIFORNIA
MRLD 19

Previous page
The ***1958 Chevrolet Bel Air Impala*** *must have been the talk of the shop-floor when it arrived on the scene in October, 1957. With its dual headlights, heavy bumper/grille and radically different rear end, the new Bel Air bore little more than a passing resemblance to the previous three years' offerings. But, overstyled or not, Chevy lovers obviously thought it was a strikingly handsome car, particularly the top-of-the-line Impala, since Chevrolet sold well over a million variations of this design in 1958. Maybe their promise of 'the road-smoothingest, nerve-soothingest ride imagineable' had something to do with it?*

Above
Functional object or 'object d'art'?

Above left
Profiled against a polarized sky above Studio City, the Impala, with all its bright metal trim, may look a shade garish or even vulgar compared to modern-day cars, but back in 1958 it was exactly what the American public wanted. Or so it was told

Left
Interior appointments were 'sports' orientated and included a deep-hub 2-spoke 'wheel, tri-tone ventilated vinyl seats, and a 'medallion' featuring crossed racing flags on the rear speaker grille

Starting with the 1958 models, cars changed even faster and in more extravagant ways than before, and the introduction of the new models became a yearly suspense drama. 'Top secret' designs, covered in canvas, were seen being trucked out of Detroit. Telephoto spy shots were 'leaked' to the press as appetizers. Then, as families across the nation sat spellbound in front of the Philco Predicta, the curtain was lifted on the future – leastways, the next twelve months. But the very profusion of designs, the unceasing novelty, provided an indication that all was not right with the system: 'planned absolescence was not getting a chance to work,' as *Business Week* put it in 1959.

Nothing aged faster than last year's fin, but that was good news for teenagers and the less affluent citizens of America. *Gerry's Cherrys* was chock-a-block with one, two and three-year-old cars which were barely run-in, and good deals on sharp wheels spelled *fun, fun, fun* for a generation which, in 1958, was dancing to Danny and the Juniors' big chart success, *At the Hop*. Long gone were the days when a boy walked his girl to the movies or spent summer nights in the porch holding hands. Now you could cruise Main Street at the weekend,

Below
Chevrolet bucked the tail fin trend in 1958, opting for 'gullwing' fenders instead. Power choices that year included the 283 Super Turbo-Fire and 348 Super Turbo-Thrust mated to either a Powerglide or Turboglide transmission. But in spite of those exotic sounding powerplants, the 1958 Bel Air was longer, wider and heavier, thus slower than its predecessor

drink root beer at the A & W and eat popcorn at the drive-in; it was West Side Story for the nation's youth, and for them the cold war was conducted on the back seat of a Chevy convertible.

Needless to say, engines grew larger and more powerful as Detroit's development engineers worked overtime in an effort to justify the marketing claims, which had become as over-inflated as the cars themselves. Buick's chrome-encrusted 1958 model, featuring a record 44 lbs worth of embellishment, was dubbed the Airborne B-58, after the bomber. It was said to represent 'a decisive break-through into a new era of transportation by land', and its engine became the B-12000 because it developed 12,000 lbs of 'thrust' behind every piston stroke. What's more, the motor was backed up by 'Flight-Pitch' Dynaflow transmission and the car floated on 'Air-Poise' suspension. But that was nothing compared to the creative copywriting which had aimed to

Above
Projectile-like door moulding says a lot about American design in the fifties

Left

The sun sets yet again, this time on a ***1958 Ford Thunderbird****. The all-new four-seater Thunderbird was described by its makers as 'the car everyone would love to own', and was voted* Motor Trend *magazine's Car of the Year. The 'Squarebird', as it became known, was bigger, heavier and cushier than the original Thunderbird, and was marketed as a comfortable sporty car for the comfortable sporty family – which proved an intelligent move. The 1959 model, in both Tudor hardtop and convertible guise, found three times more buyers than its 1957 counterpart. This 1958 still had its original 300 bhp 352 cubic inch engine backed up by a Ford-O-Matic automatic transmission*

Above

1958 Edsel Citation: *the unmistakable Edsel, the product of a short-lived Ford division named after Henry Ford's late son, represents one of the greatest industrial disasters of the twentieth century – so much so that the name 'Edsel' is now an officially recognised synonym for 'loser'. The model was designed in 1955 and finally introduced to the public in September 1957, in an attempt to halt the exodus of the 'nouveau riches' to more costly GM marques (market research had shown that the vast majority of Ford owners who wished to enhance their social status by trading up into the middle price bracket, switched to Oldsmobile, Buick or Pontiac). The Edsel was to be the embodiment of a dream already existing in the minds of prospective buyers, but proved to be a woeful misreading of the consumer psyche. After heavy marketing hype in which 200,000 sales were predicted in the first year, Edsel sold just 110,000 cars prior to the cessation of the division in November 1959 at an estimated loss of $450 million to Ford. That front end, which has been likened to many things, must surely take much of the blame . . .*

Above
Car's the Star, *an enterprising outfit in Kansas, Missouri, have cashed in on the current boom in nostalgia by producing this unique line in furniture. Most of the raw material comes from the wrecker's yard, but once transformed sells for around $12,000 apiece. This used to be a 1958 Cadillac. It is now the focus of attention in National's reception area*

sell the previous year's Dodge: 'It tames a tornado of torque. It breaks through the vibration barrier. It is swept-wing mastery in motion. It unleashes a hurricane of power! Aerodynamics has unleashed the thundering power of a new aircraft-type V8 engine.' No engineering development went unnoticed as production cars came closer to resembling dream cars, and the dream was re-written yearly.

By the end of 1958, just about every American car manufacturer had copied Cadillac's fin and quad headlight look, the latter having been first previewed in late 1956. Cadillacs featured most of the stylistic clichés of the fifties (tensed wraparound windshields, protruding 'Dagmar' bumpers, and so on) before other makes, since it was the flagship division of General Motors' colossal empire; the division which had first employed Harley Earl back in the twenties. The end of Earl's career, and the end of the most flamboyant era in car design, came when he retired from GM in 1959. After having almost single-handedly dictated the style of the American automobile for more than thirty years, he used all his power and influence and somehow pursuaded the bean-counters at GM to put his 1959 Cadillac design – the quintessential late fifties American car – into production. It was a wildly creative exercise with no boundaries imposed; a lavish overstatement of power, luxury and the glamour of success; Harley Earl's parting statement. But how curious that the proginator of so much automotive extravagance should build and keep for his own personal use after retirement a Ferrari-style, Oldsmobile-based roadster with none of the styling traits for which he had been famous.

Even before the unveiling of the 1959 Cadillac, *Look* magazine had asked 'Is the buying public tired of the big, luxurious "living room on

Below
Every California Classic is given the once-over after each rental to keep it in good running order. MRLD 86, an Edsel, required rear end work, while MRLD II, the rarely-stationary 1957 Vette, was in for a brake job and yet another major service. The 1960 Caddy was about to join the hard-working fleet

Left
Enormous round tail lights help to produce a startling effect at the rear

Right
Floating star-like ornaments in a full-width grille did nothing to spoil the Galaxie's overall image

Below
*Many consider the **1959 Ford Galaxie** to be the most attractive Ford of the fifties. The car had an elegance that was recognised with a Gold Medal for Exceptional Styling at the Brussels World Fair, and displayed comparative restraint when others were being made to look as if they were capable of inter-galactic travel and supersonic speed. Around the same time as this car was manufactured, Marilyn Monroe was making the movie 'Some Like It Hot' with Jack Lemon and Tony Curtis*

Below
'Not' a casual snapshot – in fact you wouldn't believe how long it took to get the Galaxie positioned within sight of those nine colossal letters . . .

wheels" styling? Is a consumer revolt in the making?' Certainly, by the turn of the decade, a degree of cynicism had begun to infect the once-optimistically motorized nation. Auto styling, especially that of the Edsel, had become the butt of jokes, and American cars were satirized by the intellectual elite as mechanical pets which had taken over their masters. Even President Eisenhower had accused Detroit of not giving the public the cars it wanted.

A national economic slump in 1958 cut deeply into domestic car sales and allowed imports, notably the Volkswagen, a firm toehold in the US market. To fend off the revolution, the Big Three intro-

duced 'compact' cars (Corvair, Falcon and Valiant) in 1959, and they sold fairly well. But the manufacturers' bet was hedged; big cars sold even better. Despite mounting protests that they symbolized the nation's wastefulness, gluttony and greed, most Americans had grown accustomed to luxury and power in their daily transportation, and they weren't about to change their expectations overnight. ■

Above
*Weighing-in at 4,545 lbs, this 18 ft 7 in long **1959 Oldsmobile Ninety-Eight** is a real 'land yacht'! In an advertisement at the time, Oldsmobile's copywriters extolled the car's 'Linear Look' and claimed it was 'aglow with bright ideas'. It featured a brand-new 394 in engine which, in the same year as the air speed record increased to 1520 mph, was said to be 'the most efficient Rocket engine yet'*

Above
The Olds shows its face in one of the select residential streets of Westwood, near UCLA. When dual headlights arrived in 1958, the face-like quality of American automobiles was suppressed as the eyes and mouth merged into a comparatively simple, horizontal combination

Left
A vast array of colourful vinyl interiors was offered, reflecting the general mood of the period. Ray-Bans are, of course, essential when driving . . .

Above
1959 Cadillac Series 62, *Sunset Boulevard, Hollywood. This is it, the pinnacle of automotive excess; the 'maxima'. Harley Earl's dictum to his styling staff in the late fifties was said to be 'Go all the way and then back off'. On this occasion, the year in which the Hollywood born-and-bred designer retired from GM, they just kept on going!*

Overleaf
With fins 42 in off the ground, the 1959 Caddy, according to one critic at the time, 'shows the misapplication of the functional forms of jet planes for aesthetic effect.' The more cynical commentators have since referred to this display of extravagance as 'GM's last laugh'

Above
Somewhat baroque split-level radiator grille comprised some 80 pieces, and there's another one at the rear . . .

Right
Could it have just landed from the Planet Cadillac, I wonder? Now there's an idea for a movie!

It may be chic, entertaining and shamelessly decadent in this day and age, but boy, does it guzzle the gas! But then you wouldn't really worry about that fact if you owned one of these cultural symbols. The very best Biarritz versions are now fetching in excess of $100,000

54
53
52
911
50
911
50
MRLD117

'The 1959 Cadillac car speaks so eloquently – in so many ways – of the man who sits at its wheel. Simply because it is a Cadillac. For instance, it indicates his high level of personal achievement. Because it is so beautiful and majestic, it bespeaks his fine sense of taste. And because it is so economical to own and to operate, it testifies to his great practical wisdom. Why not visit your dealer tomorrow and arrange to let a new Cadillac tell its wonderful story about you!'
(1959 Cadillac ad headlined 'Cadillac . . . universal symbol of achievement')
Location: Playa Del Ray. (Who said 'It never rains in California?')

National's Classics are washed after every rental.

Optional Sonomatic push-button radio

Sonomatic
STATIONS
BUICK
BASS
TREBLE

Right
Buick has always symbolized a certain upward mobility (professional types who have moved up from a Chevy, or perhaps an Olds), but back in 1959/60 the fancy 225s appeared to lack much of the continuity with Buick's past and got a rather cool reception in the showrooms – making them all the more desirable today, needless to say

Left
As well as the radio with an electric antenna, the 225 convertible buyer had the option of such things as air conditioning, bucket seats, dual-speed wipers, rear seat speaker, tissue dispenser, litter basket, and so on. Power brakes, power steering, power windows and power seats, and leather upholstery, were all included in the asking price of $4,192 (exactly mid-way between a Chevrolet Impala and a Series 62 Cadillac)

Above
I came across this location by accident – well, almost. Apart from a few non-starters, this was the only Classic that let me down, the brakes went on La Cienega Boulevard, near Beverly Hills. Thankfully, Buick introduced a step-on parking brake into their 1960 models which enabled me to crawl a few hundred yards into the car park at Ed Debevic's fifties-style diner (meatloaf recommended), where I found this graphic façade. What a caper . . .

Overleaf
One of the many murals in Los Angeles, just off Hollywood Boulevard

PRESCRIPTIO

80

—THE— KENNEDY YEARS

Post-war America had been a nation without shame. It had assumed and accepted leadership in all fields from fashion to commerce to diplomacy, and the excitement of a time of hopes and dreams fulfilled had provided a good life which, in some cases, was very good indeed. Its lifestyle, products and ideas were emulated all over the world, and John F. Kennedy, speaking as a candidate for the 1960 presidential election, described the era as 'the greatest period of progress in history'. But as the new decade dawned, there was the stark realization that the world was not the same place it had been ten years ago. There was insurrection in both the Southern states, while in Cuba, Fidel Castro had ousted the Batista regime described by Kennedy as

__1960 Pontiac Catalina,__ two truckers and their rigs. Pontiac's image as a producer of rather staid family cars vanished altogether in the sixties when Pontiac, Michigan became the home of high performance. This 389-engined convertible may not fall into the 'hot collectible' category, but the truck drivers were impressed nonetheless

WHITE

Above
The ubiquitous school bus adds a touch of colour to the car named after a beautiful island two hours from Long Beach, a popular excursion point for tourists. In 1960, convertible sales in the US accounted for roughly $4\frac{1}{2}$ per cent of the total car market, though little more than a decade later the figure was less than one per cent

Right
The previous-year Pontiac had featured not one but two sharp-edged fins on each rear fender. Styling – by definition an American approach to design in which a product's appearance is moulded for the purpose of increasing sales – was taking on a more restrained look

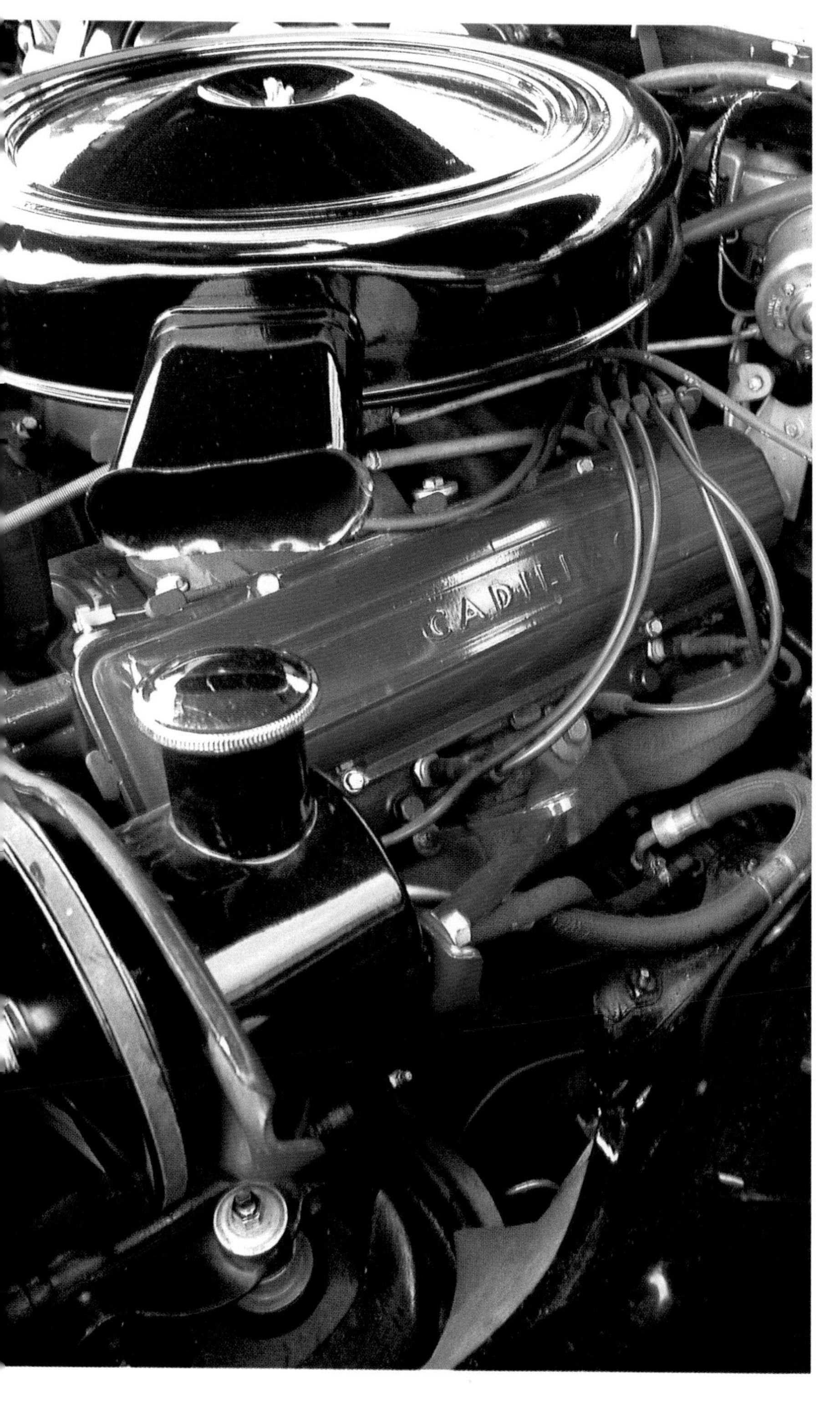

Cadillac's huge mill had to act like a small power station in order to supply the push-button electric everything.

'one of the most bloody and repressive dictatorships in the long history of Latin America'. It had been American backed. It was no time to be selling tomorrow's world today, but Detroit had no choice; the public had grown used to the idea of the 'disposable' car.

In a ten year span, the American automobile had grown in size, luxury and power to a degree beyond the imagination in 1949, though by the time J. F. Kennedy was inaugurated as the youngest-ever President of the United States, its imposing dimensions were no longer a novelty; the great tail fin war was over. Cars became less flamboyant about their girth and weight, and 'restraint' finally entered the stylists' vocabulary albeit relative to the peak of extravagance displayed on the 1959 models. Harley Earl's departure from the industry probably had something to do with it, likewise the voices calling for a more balanced approach to transportation. Not that they received much joy in the corporate *engineering* departments.

In 1950, a Chevrolet cost around $1,500 and came with either a 90 hp or a 105 hp six cylinder engine, with a choice of three-speed manual or Powerglide transmission. By 1960, the price had doubled but the Chevy buyer had a choice of no less than eight engines – a 135 hp six or a 170/185 hp 283 cubic inch V8 as stan-

*Out of the city and into the desert, we're on the road to 'Vegas in a **1960 Dodge Phoenix**. Dodge models for the new decade featured unitary body/chassis construction for the first time. They were relatively light, and offered good performance with reasonable economy, as well as the innovative push-button transmission first introduced in 1956. Norm Thatcher drove a supercharged hardtop Phoenix at Bonneville in 1960 and achieved a record speed of 192 mph, as almost 9,000 convertibles rolled off the production line*

CALIFORNIA
MRLD 85

Above
As many cars gained a friendlier look, the 1960 Dodge maintained quite a fierce toothy image, though it did change the following year

Main picture
Phoenix in the desert. The Mojave Desert and the southerly Sonoran Desert comprise the bulk of Southern California, and this shot was taken in the Mojave, a few miles east of Barstow. The California desert reaches beyond Las Vegas to the borders of Nevada and Arizona in the east, extends south to the Mexican border and beyond, and a narrow section stretches northeast beyond the eastern slope of the Sierra Nevada. The Mojave, far from being a uniform wilderness, is punctuated by sharp, truncated mountain ranges, dry canyons, playas and plateaus, and is filled with numerous life forms and communities. And that late-afternoon light is just amazing!

Above
Tail lights are enclosed in a chrome bezel which was likened at the time to the intake scoop of an F-86 Sabre Jet

K1484

Left

1961 Corvette: the twin-headlight Corvette was more than an exciting sports car in the early sixties, it was an exciting way of life. As the star of the weekly TV series, Route 66, *the Corvette was seen by millions of Americans as a means of escape into a world of adventure, and those who were fortunate enough to own one in real life were looked upon with envious eyes. 'Fuelie' versions, when equipped with a stump-pulling 4.11.1 rear end ratio, turned the quarter mile in 14.2 seconds at 99 mph*

dard, a 230 hp Super Turbo-Fire V8, a 250 hp Turbo-Thrust V8, a 280 hp Super Turbo-Thrust V8, a 300 hp Special Turbo-Thrust V8, and a 335 hp Special Super Turbo-Thrust V8 – and five different transmissions! Over this ten year period, Chevrolet's power-to-weight ratio increased three-fold, while the 0–60 acceleration time was cut from around 20 seconds in 1950 to less than 7 seconds for the 1960 model fitted with the 335 hp engine. What's more, this neck-snapping performance was bargain priced – roughly $9 per horse, compared to nearly $17 in 1950. The same rates applied to Ford and Plymouth.

What had once been run-of-the-mill family sedans were, by 1962, out-and-out street racers. Chevy's monster-motored 409 Impala, Ford's 406 inch Galaxy and Plymouth's 383 Fury each had more than 400 horsepower under the hood and would out-run any exotic Italian sportscar on the street. Cadillacs, Lincolns and Chryslers, meanwhile, gained around 1,000 lbs from 1950 to 1960 and were now superior in size, weight and price only.

Above
While a good many young people were scouring used-car markets for power-packed 1955–57 Chevys, the high-performance **1961 Chevrolet Impala** *arrived on the showroom floor. Tail fins had gone forever and for the first time buyers had the option of the Turbo-Fire 409, then rated at 360 horsepower. Though only a handful went for the monster motor the first year, many thousands felt its now-legendary punch in 1962 and the Beach Boys even wrote a song about it. Chevrolet was King of the Street*

Left
This factory push-botton radio put $62 on the price of a V8 Impala convertible, to just over $3k

*The **1962 Cadillac Series 62** was advertised as 'the most luxurious, most superbly crafted automobile in all of motordom'! The sweeping tail fins and chromey front end typified the Cadillac look of the late fifties and early sixties. The Series 62 was almost 19 ft long, weighed more than two tons and boasted 325 bhp from a 390 cubic inch V8. Included on its long list of luxury features were power steering, power brakes, automatic transmission, dual speed windscreen wipers and washers, and a remote control door mirror. Rubberized front and rear coil springs, which had replaced the trouble prone air suspension system a year previously, made for the smoothest ride imaginable to and from the Royal Laundry in Pasadena*

LAUNDRY DRIVE-IN
477

Above
$5,500 new; around double the price in A1 condition today. What a lot of car for the money

American cars of the early sixties mirrored all the comfort and convenience of the average suburban home on Wendy's Way. Carpeting and upholstery were as elegant as that in the living room, while air conditioning provided a cool, pleasant environment and peace from the traffic noise outside. Almost every manufacturer offered power steering, brakes, windows, seats and so on, along with tinted glass, variable speed wipers, remote control door mirrors, cigar lighters, map lights and suchlike. Now, for a few hundred dollars more, Everyman could boast the kind of in-car features and under-hood power that was once exclusive to the prestige car buyer.

The shift in emphasis from fins and chrome to power and performance was echoed in pop music of the early sixties. By then, the hard edge of Rock'n'Roll had been rounded off, just like the cars' fins. Groups like the Beach Boys, Jan and Dean and the Rondells sang about hot rodding and surfing as young Californians searched for the perfect wave. However, by the time the Beatles arrived on the scene and the once clean-cut bobby-soxers were drafted into a war they were told

not to win, good old American traditions and values poured out of the window like confetti. It was the dawning of the Age of Aquarius, and the chrome-encrusted symbols of the nation's post-war indulgence were considered 'phoney' and 'irrelevant'.

The time had come to be relevant, to 'give a damn', to care about the human race and the world that existed beyond the backyard. As the war babies' revolt turned psychedelic, the newly committed began to flaunt lapel badges in favour of everything from the mini-skirt to the Maharishi, and everyone from

Above
1962 Chrysler 300H: *the luxurious, high-performance, letter-series 300 was introduced in 1955 and thereafter received the next letter in the alphabet with each passing model year. It was nothing short of a factory hot rod, with specially tuned suspension, heavy duty brakes and a leather interior. As for the engine, the 'H' version came standard with the top-of-the-line Chrysler 413 cubic inch V8 with 10-to-1 compression, solid cam and dual 4-barrel carbs. This set-up was good for 380 bhp at 5,200 rpm and 450 lb/ft of torque at 3,600 rpm. What's more, if you could prove to a dealer that you had sufficient experience in either drag or roundy-round racing, you could order a 1962 'H' with an even wilder 405 horse motor . . . This beautiful 54,000 mile example (when I parted with it) was one of only 337, 300H convertibles produced in 1962, and it was once owned by Karen Carpenter, the late singer*

Above
The worst aspect of renting a California Classic is deciding whether or not to ever return it to the LAX facility. This Chrysler places big demands on your sense of honesty, believe me!

Right
Fifties flash is more than evident in the Chrysler's dash – but which buttons flipped the discs?

Timothy Leary to Ho Chi Minh. But, certainly prior to the assassination which stunned the world in 1963, Detroit continued to churn out big cars for 'the establishment' which were loaded with power and creature comforts. Similarly churned out was a range of compacts which, infected with the virus of the late fifties, grew a little larger and a little more powerful each year.

The early sixties were the heyday of the convertible in America, during which time the glamorous bodystyle enjoyed a six per cent share of the overall car market. Production levels peaked in 1965, which, not coincidentally, was the year Ralph Nader's book *Unsafe at Any Speed* was first published.

10 20 30 40 50 60 70 80 90
BRAKE
TEMP
ANTENNA
DOME LIGHT

Above
With its canted quad headlights, the 'H' was the last but one of the 300 series to be styled under the supervision of Virgil Exner, who by this time was known as Virgil 'Excess'. The '300' designation originally represented the horsepower rating of the model's 331 cubic inch hemi-head engine. The following year, 1956, saw this bhp figure upped to 335, and by 1960 a souped-up 413 inch Wedge-head put out exactly 400 horses; the highest of any production car in the world. The high-priced 300 series changed Chrysler's image just as the small block V8 changed Chevrolet's, but it was discontinued after 1965 as mega-performance had become the order of the day for every manufacturer

Right
Two enormous round tail lights, looking like jet afterburners, replaced the six-light arrangement of the 1960 T-Bird, while the 1964–1966 model featured full width housings and sequential turn signals

Nader, leading consumer advocate and arch enemy of the American auto industry, exposed Detroit's unlimited horsepower regime as profiting at the expense of public safety. He castigated their cynical neglect of effort to make cars more crashworthy, and urged the passing of federal and state legislation to bring pressure to bear. As consumer protection and conservation movements condemned the bullish exuberance of the late fifties' design philosophy, the roles of form and function returned to a more logical relationship and American car styling lost much of its primitive dynamism.

The automobile industry, indeed America as a whole, would never be quite the same again. ■

HUGHES

1963 Ford Thunderbird Sports Roadster: *while convertibles had never accounted for more than about an eighth of post-1957 Thunderbird sales, they were important image builders. For 1961's third generation design, Ford began considering how it might satisfy the small but vocal demand for an open top two-seater, in the original T-Bird vein. Designer Bud Kaufman came up with a simple but striking solution; a fibreglass tonneau with faired-in headrests which covered the normal convertible's rear seat area. He also overcame fitting problems so that the soft top could be raised or lowered with the cover in place. The Sports Roadster was the only four-seater production car that became a two-seater, but at a whopping $5,439 in 1962 – $650 more than a regular convertible – it attracted few buyers. Just 455 in 1963, to be precise*

Above
The rare Bird, with its severely-pointed profile and wire wheels, was shot at a freeway construction site near LAX. Angelenos knock the over-crowded freeways, but they are a vital part of the California Dream

Left
After 1963, the T-Bird became more of a luxury car than a Grand Tourer, but the third generation model retained much of the 'personal' cachet which had originated in 1955. This image held strong appeal for the well-heeled who would never have been satisfied with a Corvette. This Roadster features an optional 'swing-away' steering wheel which shifts sideways about ten inches, thereby allowing easy access to the low-slung driver's seat

Right
At the flick of a switch, the rear deck opens, the steel centre panel flips over and descends into the trunk, and the top folds forward. Neat!

Cruisin' Bev' Hills in a first generation **Ford Mustang**. *Ford launched the Mustang in April, 1964 and it became the biggest single success story since the Model T; a sporty car with a look almost everyone liked at a price almost anyone could afford. Moreover, it was available with a myriad of options that could render it an economical 6-cylinder grocery-getter or a competitive street-dragster, a luxury compact or a 'Gran Turismo'. This car was all things to all men and women and it sold like hot cakes – more than one and a quarter million units in the first two model years. Much of the credit for this achievement which literally transformed product thinking in Detroit, can be attributed to Lee A. Iacocca, an engineer-turned-car salesman who worked his way up from an obscure sales position to vice-president and general manager of Ford Division in five years, and went on to become President of Ford Motor Company. The convertible pictured here is an immaculate 1966 model with less than 40,000 miles on its original 'two-eighty-nine'*

The name 'Mustang', meaning a wild horse, connoted cowboys, prairies, the romantic Wild West. It was easy to spell and, as one Ford ad man said, 'It was as American as all hell'. So successful was the Mustang that a whole assortment of similar cars, by competitive manufacturers, came to be known as 'pony cars' or, in other words, cars in the original Mustang image

This small-block 'Stang is loaded with sought after options, including a four-outlet air conditioning unit, centre console, 8-track cartridge player and a 'pony' interior package consisting of embossed upholstery and several touches of simulated walnut. So 'Sixties'!

The famous Beverly Hills Hotel on Sunset Boulevard, built in 1912, is a luxurious example of Mission architecture set back amid 12 acres of the lushest, most valuable land in Southern California. We never did see Joan Collins, but we certainly saw 'how the other half live . . .'